Great African Americans

Frederick Douglass

Leader against slavery

Revised Edition

Patricia and Fredrick McKissack

Series Consultant
Dr. Russell L. Adams, Chairman
Department of Afro-American Studies, Howard University

Enslow Publishers, Inc.

40 Industrial Road	PO Box 38
Box 398	Aldershot
Berkeley Heights, NJ 07922	Hants GU12 6BP
USA	UK

http://www.enslow.com

To Blake

Revised edition of *Frederick Douglass: Leader Against Slavery* © 1991

Library of Congress Cataloging-in-Publication Data

McKissack, Pat, 1944–
    Frederick Douglass : leader against slavery / Patricia and Fredrick McKissack.— Rev. ed.
        p. cm. — (Great African Americans)
    Includes index.
    ISBN-10: 0-7660-1696-X
    1. Douglass, Frederick, 1817?–1895—Juvenile literature. 2. Abolitionists—United States—Biography—
Juvenile literature. 3. Afro-American abolitionists—Biography—Juvenile literature. 4. Antislavery
movements—United States—History—19th century—Juvenile literature. [1. Douglass, Frederick,
1817?–1895. 2. Abolitionists. 3. Afro-Americans—Biography.] I. McKissack, Fredrick. II. Title.
    E449.D75 M378   2001
    973.8'092—dc21   00-012415

ISBN-13: 978-0-7660-1696-5

Printed in the United States of America

10 9 8

To Our Readers: We have done our best to make sure all Internet addresses in this book were active and appropriate when we went to press. However, the author and the publisher have no control over and assume no liability for the material available on those Internet sites or on other Web sites they may link to. Any comments or suggestions can be sent by e-mail to comments@enslow.com or to the address on the back cover.

Every effort has been made to locate all copyright holders of materials used in this book.
If any errors or omissions have occurred, corrections will be made in future editions of this book.

Illustration Credits: Courtesy National Park Service, p. 25; Frederick Douglass Museum and Cultural Center, p. 18; Library of Congress, pp. 3, 4, 9, 10T, 13, 14, 15, 19, 21, 23B, 24, 26; Missouri Historical Society, St. Louis, by Thomas Satter White, p. 6; Missouri Historical Society, St. Louis, by Kurz Allison, p. 20; Moorland-Spingarn Research Center, Howard University, p. 12; National Archives, p. 23T; Photography and Prints Division, Schomburg Center for Research in Black Culture, The New York Public Library, Astor, Lenox and Tilden Foundations, pp. 7, 27; Reproduced from *American Advertising Posters of the Nineteenth Century from the Bella C. Landauer Collection of the New-York Historical Society* published by Dover Publications, Inc., 1976, p. 16.

Cover Illustrations: Courtesy National Park Service; Frederick Douglass Museum and Cultural Center; Library of Congress; Moorland-Spingarn Research Center, Howard University; National Archives.

TaBLe of
CONTENTS

Frederick Douglass
February 14, 1817(?)–February 20, 1895

CHAPTER 1

Alone!

Harriet Bailey was a slave. All her children were slaves, too. On (or near) Valentine's Day in 1817 or 1818, Harriet gave birth to a son. She named him Frederick Augustus Washington Bailey.

When the baby was only one week old, Harriet was ordered back to work. But Frederick wasn't left alone. He was sent to live with his Grandmama Betsey and Grandpa Isaac.

Little Fred didn't see his mother very much.

**As if they were animals, black men, women, and children
were sold in public places as slaves.**

She worked far away. Fred was happy until he was about eight years old.

At that time Grandmama Betsey took him to the main plantation, in Tuckahoe, Maryland. She had been told to leave him there. Why, why? he cried.

The boy didn't understand slavery. Slaves had to do what their masters said.

The cook took care of all the children at the main plantation. She was a slave, too. Still, she beat Fred when he cried.

One day the cook was going to beat Fred. But Harriet came in. "Never hit my child again," the angry mother said. The cook ran out of the room.

Harriet hugged her son. She fed him. She sang to him. Then it was time for her to go. Harriet had to do what her master said.

Fred never saw his mother again. Harriet died soon after that visit.

Fred was alone.

Like Frederick Douglass, some blacks had lighter skin because their fathers were white.

CHAPTER 2

Never!

fred lived at the main plantation for a year. The cook beat him almost every day.

Then Fred was sent to be a house slave for Sophia and Hugh Auld.

Sophia Auld was a kind woman. She taught her son and Fred how to read and write.

Then one day Fred read for Hugh Auld. Mr. Auld was very, very angry. "Never teach a slave to read," said Mr. Auld. "He won't want to stay a slave."

Mrs. Auld stopped teaching Fred how to read. But Fred didn't stop reading.

When Fred was sixteen, he was sent back to the main plantation in Tuckahoe. Thomas Auld was his master.

Fred wouldn't act like a slave. So Auld sent him to a slave-breaker. Fred was made to work from morning until night. All he had to do was act like a slave. But Fred said, "Never!" He stayed with the slave-breaker for almost a year.

Cruel masters often whipped their slaves to make them obey.

9

$200 Reward.

RANAWAY from the subscriber, on the night of Thursday, the 30th of Sepember,

FIVE NEGRO SLAVES,

To-wit: one Negro man, his wife, and three children.

The man is a black negro, full height, very erect, his face a little thin. He is about forty years of age, and calls himself *Washington Reed*, and is known by the name of Washington. He is probably well dressed, possibly takes with him an ivory headed cane, and is of good address. Several of his teeth are gone.

Mary, his wife, is about thirty years of age, a bright mulatto woman, and quite stout and strong.

The oldest of the children is a boy, of the name of FIELDING, twelve years of age, a dark mulatto, with heavy eyelids. He probably wore a new cloth cap.

MATILDA, the second child, is a girl, six years of age, rather a dark mulatto, but a bright and smart looking child.

MALGOLM, the youngest, is a boy, four years old, a lighter mulatto than the last, and about equally as bright. He probably also wore a cloth cap. If examined, he will be found to have a swelling at the navel. Washington and Mary have lived at or near St. Louis, with the subscriber, for about 15 years.

It is supposed that they are making their way to Chicago, and that a white man accompanies them, that they will travel chiefly at night, and most probably in a covered wagon.

A reward of $150 will be paid for their apprehension, so that I can get them, if taken within one hundred miles of St. Louis, and $200 if taken beyond that, and secured so that I can get them, and other reasonable additional charges, if delivered to the subscriber, or to THOMAS ALLEN, Esq., at St. Louis, Mo. The above negroes, for the last few years, have been in possession of Thomas Allen, Esq., of St. Louis.

WM. RUSSELL.

LOUIS, Oct. 1, 1847.

One day Fred fought back. He stopped the slave-breaker from beating him. Auld and the slave-breaker had tried to make Fred a willing slave. Now they knew it would never work.

Thomas Auld sent Frederick back to Hugh and Sophia. By that time, Fred knew that he was going to run away.

CHAPTER 3

Run!

I t was 1838. Frederick was eighteen years old and very good-looking.

He met Anna, a free black woman who lived in Baltimore, Maryland. He loved Anna and wanted to marry her. But Frederick wouldn't ask—not until he was free, too.

Freedom was always on his mind. He wanted to run. *Run! Run!* His friends said wait. He needed a plan.

After many months of planning, Frederick was ready to run. At last the day came. Dressed as a free sailor, he rode the train to Delaware. Blacks who were not slaves had to carry special papers—called free papers—all the time. Frederick's free papers belonged to a friend. If anyone checked, he would be in trouble. But no one checked closely.

Many of his friends were free—and Frederick pledged that one day he would be free too.

Then, from Delaware, Frederick took a boat to Philadelphia. *Run, Fred, run!*

From Philadelphia, he went to New York. *Run, Fred, run!*

On September 4, 1838, Frederick was in a free state. He changed his name

12

"The Fugitive's Song" was written in honor of Frederick Douglass. *Fugitive* is another word for a runaway.

13

to Frederick Augustus Douglass. He hoped slave catchers would not find him.

Right away, he sent for Anna. They were married in New York. Soon, the happy couple moved to New Bedford, Massachusetts. Frederick got a job working on ships.

It didn't take long for Fred to join the abolitionists. These were people who wanted to end slavery.

Frederick spoke out against slavery all over the North. He even wrote his own life story.

Frederick and Anna, above, had five children: Rosetta, Lewis Henry, Frederick Jr., Charles, and Annie.

Then he had to run again. Slave hunters would be coming to take him back to his master. *Run! Run!*

Fred said good-bye to his wife and children. Then he hurried off to England.

14

Two years later, on December 5, 1846, Frederick was truly freed. Friends had bought his freedom. He came back to the United States in 1847 with his own free papers. He never had to run again.

Runaway slaves could be forced to go back to their masters.

To earn money, Frederick helped build and fix ships.

CHAPTER 4

Freedom!

frederick Douglass was a free man. But what about all those who were still slaves? He believed all people should be free. That would be his life's work.

The Douglasses moved to Rochester, New York. There, Frederick started *The North Star*, a weekly newspaper. *The North Star* was the light in the sky that runaways followed to freedom.

Abraham Lincoln was elected president of the United States in November 1860. South Carolina

Douglass believed the only way slavery would end was through war. Some abolitionists agreed with him. Some did not.

said it was no longer a part of the United States in December 1860. Other states in the South followed. The Civil War began in April 1861.

In 1863 Lincoln freed the slaves. Douglass wept when he heard the news. "What [Lincoln] has done is to [get rid of] a terrible evil that has [had hold of] this country. . . ."

Douglass met with President Lincoln in the White House. Douglass asked that black men be allowed to join the North's army. They had the right to fight for freedom.

In 1847, Frederick started a newspaper with articles against slavery.

Two of Douglass's sons were among the first black men to join the Union Army. Other black men followed. The African-American soldiers won many medals for bravery during the war.

Later Douglass pushed for equal pay. "Black

Black soldiers fought and died at Fort Wagner during the Civil War. Douglass pushed for black soldiers to get the same pay as white soldiers.

and white soldiers die the same," he said. "They should be paid the same." At last, both black and white soldiers were paid the same.

The war ended in 1865. President Lincoln was killed soon afterward. Douglass was very sad. He said, "It is a dark time for us all."

In 1863, President Abraham Lincoln freed all slaves.

CHAPTER 5

Hero!

When the Civil War ended, Frederick Douglass was called a hero. He had not been a soldier. But he had been fighting to end slavery for so long.

Some people thought Douglass's work was over. Instead, he tried new things. For a while he was president of a bank. And he also worked for women's rights.

Finally, the Douglasses closed *The North Star* and moved to Washington, D.C. President

Rutherford B. Hayes had asked Douglass to be the marshal of the District of Columbia. In later years, he was chosen by other presidents to serve the government, too.

The Douglass home was called Cedar Hill. It was a happy place. People came to visit all the time. Anna always made their house a fun place. Their children were grown up. They had children of their own. It was full of happy sounds and good smells. Douglass was never too busy to hug a grandchild. Family was always very important to him.

Anna died after being ill. Once more Frederick was alone. He had never liked being alone. Soon he

Douglass, above, wrote three books about his life. This was the first.

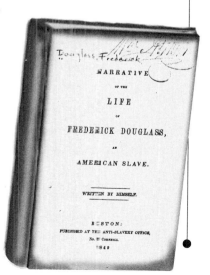

23

married a second time. Many people felt he should not have married again. But he was happy.

Frederick was not happy about the way things were changing. By the 1890s, unfair laws were being passed. Black people were losing their rights. Frederick Douglass was old and tired. But he still spoke up for freedom and justice. He always would.

Two of Douglass's sons—Lewis Henry, left, and Frederick Jr., right—pose with his grandson Joseph Douglass. Joseph became the first African-American violinist to perform in concert tours.

He spoke to a large group in Washington, D.C., on February 20, 1895. Later that evening, Frederick Douglass died. A great American hero was gone.

Douglass will always be remembered as an abolitionist. He had been a slave. But he could

Douglass with his second wife, Helen, on a visit to Niagara Falls.

Frederick Douglass's house, Cedar Hill, is now open as a museum in Washington, D.C.

never understand how one person could own another.

In a speech he gave one Fourth of July, he said, "There is no way a nation can call itself free and accept slavery." We know now that his words are true.

Runaway slave Frederick Douglass was famous for speaking out to end slavery. He was a great American hero.

timeLine

1817(?) ~ Born a slave in Talbot County, Maryland.

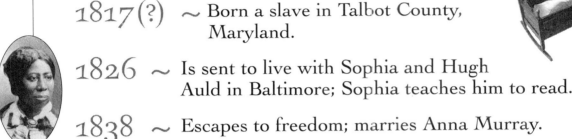

1826 ~ Is sent to live with Sophia and Hugh Auld in Baltimore; Sophia teaches him to read.

1838 ~ Escapes to freedom; marries Anna Murray.

1841 ~ Makes first speech against slavery.

1845 ~ Publishes *Narrative of the Life of Frederick Douglass: An American Slave*.

1847 ~ Publishes *The North Star*, a newspaper against slavery.

1855 ~ Publishes *My Bondage and My Freedom*.

1861 ~ Meets with President Lincoln to protest the treatment of African-American soldiers.

1877 ~ Becomes U.S. Marshal of Washington, D.C.

1881 ~ Publishes *Life and Times of Frederick Douglass*.

1884 ~ Marries Helen Pitts.

1889 ~ Becomes Consul General to Haiti.

1895 ~ Dies February 20 in Washington, D.C.

WORDS TO KNOW

abolitionist—A person who wanted to end (abolish) slavery in the United States.

bravery—An act that shows courage. Standing up to fear.

Civil War—A war fought within one country. In the United States, the Civil War was fought between states in the North and the South from 1861 to 1865.

freedom—The power to make your own choices and decisions.

free papers—Papers showing that a person was not owned.

free state—A state that did not allow slavery.

government—A group that runs a country.

marshal of the District of Columbia—A law officer of the capital of the United States of America.

master—A ruler or a person who controls another. Someone who owns slaves is called a master.

plantation—A very large farm.

president—The leader of a country or group.

29

WORDS TO KNOW

runaway—A slave who ran away to the North, where he or she could live in freedom.

slave—A person who is owned by another. That person can be bought or sold.

slave-breaker—Someone hired to beat slaves and teach them to obey or fear a master.

slave hunter—Someone who, for money, looked for runaway slaves and took them back to their masters.

Union Army—The army that fought for the North in the Civil War.

Washington, D.C.—The city where the United States government is located. D.C. stands for District of Columbia.

White House—The house where the president of the United States lives.

Learn more about Frederick Douglass

Books

Adler, David A. *A Picture Book of Frederick Douglass*. New York, N.Y.: Holiday House, 1993.

Bennett, Evelyn. *Frederick Douglass and the War Against Slavery*. Brookfield, Conn.: Millbrook Press, 1994.

McLoone, Margo. *Frederick Douglass: A Photo-Illustrated Biography*. Danbury, Conn.: Children's Press, 1997.

Weidt, Maryann N. *Voice of Freedom: A Story about Frederick Douglass*. Minneapolis, Minn.: Carolrhoda Books, 2001.

Internet Addresses

Frederick Douglass Museum & Hall of Fame for Caring Americans
Biography, timeline, photo gallery
<http://www.nahc.org/fd/index.html>

Frederick Douglass National Historic Site
Biography, historical sites
<http://www.nps.gov/archive/frdo/freddoug.html>

index